Revival Now

A Jesus Awakening

James Burns

WITH **Tom Phillips**, EDITOR

BroadStreet
P U B L I S H I N G

BroadStreet Publishing® Group, LLC
Savage, Minnesota, USA
BroadStreetPublishing.com

Revival Now: A Jesus Awakening

Copyright © 2018 Jesus Now Awakening, Inc.

ISBN 978-1-4245-5642-7 (softcover)
ISBN 978-1-4245-5643-4 (e-book)

Stock or custom editions of BroadStreet Publishing titles may be purchased in bulk for educational, business, ministry, fundraising, or sales promotional use. For information, please email info@broadstreetpublishing.com.

Cover by Chris Garborg at garborgdesign.com
Interior by Katherine Lloyd at theDESKonline.com

Printed in the United States of America

18 19 20 21 22 5 4 3 2 1

Contents

Foreword

Periodically in the history of the Christian Church, a work is produced which transcends time. *Revivals, Their Laws and Leaders* by James Burns was written in 1909 and last published in 1960. Though it is out of print, portions of the book, especially the sections on "The Laws of Revival," are so pertinent today that they cry out for editing and republishing.

"If my people, who are called by my name, will humble themselves and pray and seek my face and turn from their wicked ways, then I will hear from heaven, and I will forgive their sin and will heal their land" (2 Chronicles 7:14 NIV).

May an expectation for true spiritual revival come as we sense in reading this wonderful spiritual treatise that the world in which we live today is ripe for a new, profound movement of God's Spirit, one that has already begun. May you be encouraged.

Sincerely,
Tom Phillips

Introduction

In Christian history, no phenomenon is more clear than the recurrence of revivals. At times, a passion for repentance sweeps across specific geographical areas. Many people who had been unaware of the supernatural become keenly aware of it. They are stopped during their jobs as their minds are gripped by a terror of wrongdoing and a fear of coming judgment. Throwing all else aside, they desperately search for a way of salvation. Having started, these movements spread like wildfire and are seemingly carried in the air. Breaking out in unexpected places, they produce a strange phenomenon and awaken forces that have lain dormant. Mostly, these movements are contained in a local geographic area, but they can spread throughout nations, with incredible results.

Since revivals are a major characteristic of Christianity, a study of church growth and survival would be worthless if it ignored the impact of revivals. In light of this, we cannot regard revivals as isolated incidents. To interpret the mind and will of God in relation to humanity, we need to look at the permanent elements of human nature and the underlying laws which shape human history. Such movements witness to us the supremacy of spiritual forces. They reveal the spiritual instincts in humankind that are often clouded by less worthwhile pursuits. They encourage faith by showing God's hand in history and in His guidance of the Church. These movements prove that God is working through His laws, for the salvation of His people, and for the world's good.

In a revival, a few, then dozens, then thousands say with David, "Though I walk in the midst of trouble, You will revive me" (Psalm 138:7 NKJV).

Revival flows from Spirit-prompted living of God's Word, and faithfulness in this journey produces Spirit-Empowered disciples. The Great Commandment Network is pleased to serve Dr. Tom Phillips and the Jesus-Now Awakening through the experiential exercises at the end of each chapter. Each set of exercises seeks to focus on one of ten specific outcomes of "Living His Word" as our daily life is more and more characterized by "walking in the Light of His truth" (John 12:35, Psalm 119:105). Additional information about the Great Commandment Network, living a Spirit-Empowered Faith, and a listing of forty Discipleship outcomes have been included in the Appendices at the back of this book.

1

The Law
of Progress

We need to acknowledge the part revivals play in God's plan as we take a broader look and see them appear in places outside of the Church. Progress, we see, occurs through revival. Any progress is like the incoming tide. Each wave is revival, going forward, receding, and being followed by another. To the onlooker it seems as if nothing is gained, but the force behind the ebb and flow is the power of the tide. So it is with the nations. One will rise and carry human progress to a zenith. Having done so, it falls back, and another replaces it. Thus, the progress of humanity is continued through successive revivals.

The same is true in all realms of human expression. When new discoveries are made, the scientific outlook captivates people's minds and other areas are put on the back burner. But nothing can totally dominate the mind. The initial force eventually subsides. After making its contribution to human knowledge and making life better by its discoveries, the movement gives way and is replaced by another in a different area.

Each outburst has its own characteristics and direction, but its nature is revival. There is an excitement in an area, a gathering of energy to leap forward, and when its strength is spent, it recedes. This is even seen in commerce. Trade depressions are succeeded by trade revivals, and in the world market there is a constant ebb and flow.

In all this, we can see God's wisdom. Revivals are necessary to push humankind to higher planes. If progress were uniform, with all aspects of life improving at once, advancement would be so slow that life would stagnate. There would be no high hopes, no eager rush forward. Progress would be imperceptible and men and women, robbed of aspirations, would give up the fight. By the breath of fresh life, God keeps the world active and keeps the heart fresh with hope. In God's purposes, no part of human nature is left unrevived. Each revival is needed for helping human nature. Their order is God's secret, the equilibrium is in His hands. Behind the ebb and flow is the unrelenting tide of His redemptive purposes. He it is who said, "Let all the world look to me for salvation!" (Isaiah 45:22 TLB).

———

An Experience from Scripture

> Then he stretched himself out on the boy three times and cried out to the Lord, 'Lord my God, let this boy's life return to him!' The Lord heard Elijah's cry, and the boy's life returned to him, and he lived. Elijah picked up the child and carried him down from the room into the house. He gave him to his mother and said, "Look, your son is alive!" Then the woman said to Elijah, "Now I know that you are a man of God and that the word of the Lord from your mouth is the truth."

> –1 KINGS 17:21–24

From death to life is most certainly progress! His Word is very much alive, active, and at work by His Spirit to revive and renew.

DO the WORD

- Live life this week expectant of His working with complete confidence that "nothing is impossible with God."

- *Holy Spirit, stir my faith this week as I specifically ask you to _____.*

A Word from Jesus

- "So if the Son sets you free, you will be free indeed" (John 8:36).

- Since He's the "same yesterday, today and forever" (Hebrews 13:8), this same historical Jesus is available today to bring added freedom into your journey!

PAUSE to Encounter Jesus

- Put yourself into this promise of freedom and celebrate that this "contemporary" Jesus is *now* active in your behalf to liberate and revive your walk with Him.

- *Jesus, I celebrate your promise of freedom and specifically in my life, I need added freedom from _____ and additional freedom to _____.*

A Cry from God's People

For this is what the high and exalted One says—he who lives forever, whose name is holy: "I live in a high and holy place, but also with the one who is contrite and lowly in spirit, to revive the spirit of the lowly and to revive the heart of the contrite."

—Isaiah 57:15

Lord Jesus, would you, by your Spirit, bring conviction to your people and begin with me. Might you vindicate your name among the nations as repentance comes upon your people. Birth godly sorrow in my heart; cleanse me; forgive me.

 Join with other Jesus-followers to cry out to the Lord for Him to bring contrition of heart to His people and that He would be exalted among the nations.

2

The Law of Spiritual Growth

Revivals are the method by which progress occurs in all other realms of human expression. In light of this, we can approach their recurrence in religion free from bias, and even scorn, which has been popularly considered the right attitude. It is in this area that the word *revival* gains a new intensity, for religion deals with the awesome and unmeasurable. It goes deep into men's and women's spiritual consciousness. As interesting as other revivals may be, they are shadows when compared with the importance of revivals in the individual and the Church. Though they occur in this mysterious realm, they are not necessarily erratic or arbitrary. The supreme discovery is that nothing is erratic in God's universe. Characteristics common to all revivals may be found.

When we examine revivals in the spiritual life, we are confronted with a mass of interesting material. Revivals are used of God to stimulate individual and corporate spiritual life and to advance spiritual education and progress. They are characterized with the same frequency and fluctuations as revivals in other areas.

First, we discover fluctuations in the common experience of men and women before decisions about Christianity are made. Let's remember back before your conversion. There were times when you were conscious of definite, spiritual influences moving you powerfully to Him. Then there were long periods in which you seemed to have no consciousness of any spiritual pressure. After months—or even years—of spiritual lethargy, the influence would return.

This ebb and flow of spiritual experience is still characteristic in life after conversion. No life is maintained at the same level. The Psalms reveal the varying nature of the divine life in the believer's heart. Caught by the inflowing wave, the writer's heart rejoices in God. Then in the trough of the wave, the psalmist cries out for help, with his heart in despair. From this, God rescues him. He is then carried forward on a new tide of joy.

This same experience characterizes all Christian church life. The spiritual life within any congregation is never constant. Each church has times of being a spiritual desert, followed by times of awakening and revival. Even in the first-century Church, the believers longed for greater manifestations of God's Word and power (Acts 4:23–31).

Progress never occurs in an unbroken sequence. The pressure of the Holy Spirit upon the life of an individual and the Church is never uniform. The reason is not difficult to discover. A constant pressure becomes a mere condition of our life. We adjust to it, without its attracting our attention, but a pressure that is occasional and variable captivates our attention. The Holy Spirit demonstrates His sovereignty in nurturing change in us and captivates our interest by varying His influence at different times, for it is by this method that the conscience is reached and the heart is won.

In the influx of the tide, there are not only tiny ripples, but also tumultuous waves and mighty breakers. In the inflowing tide of human spiritual progress there is the same variety of waves. There are revivals which affect the individual. There are larger movements which affect separate congregations, and even larger ones that affect whole geographical areas and spread beyond.

This history of revivals reveals large movements, infrequent in their appearance, but monumental in their character. They change life's conditions and deeply alter the history of the world. In looking at some of these movements, we discover certain laws which govern their activity. How they work becomes more apparent, the effect more convincing and overpowering. For what is common to all great movements is present in small ones.

―――――――

An Experience from Scripture

And we all, who with unveiled faces contemplate the Lord's glory, are being transformed into his image with ever-increasing glory, which comes from the Lord, who is the Spirit.

―2 Corinthians 3:18

Give thanks for the hope and promise of transformation. Praise Him for His love that is committed to NOT leave us the way we are and for His kindness that draws us to repentance.

DO the WORD

- Celebrate and give thanks for His promise of transformation from glory to glory.

- *Lord, I celebrate the growth you have brought into my life. I once struggled so much with*

_____ *but your Spirit and grace have changed me so that I now* _____.

A Word from Jesus

- "When Jesus saw him lying there and learned that he had been in this condition for a long time, he asked him, 'Do you want to get well?'" (John 5:6).

- Allow this question often to probe your heart and life. "Do you want to get well?" It's the challenge of personal responsibility. Will I say a resounding YES! Am I sick and tired of being sick and tired?

PAUSE to Encounter Jesus

- Say YES to the Spirit's probing if you are ready for additional growth, change, renewal, and revival. "Do YOU want to get well?" Jesus waits for your answer as He did for this man's. Remain silent, and He will pass by you. Speak up, yield to Him, and transformation will come.

- "For as many as are the promises of God, in Him they are yes" (2 Corinthians 1:20).

- To this One who holds the promise of spiritual growth and revival, my heart says a resounding YES! I wish to be revived!

17

A Cry from God's People

Turn my eyes away from worthless things;
preserve my life according to your word.
Fulfill your promise to your servant, so that
you may be feared.

–PSALM 119:37–38

Revival in your ways is my need and hope.
Your ways and thoughts are higher than
mine. By your Spirit, lead me away from the
vanity of this world, especially my tendency
to _____. I yield to you that I might
walk on the narrow road that leads to life
abundant.

Live the Word W-1:
Frequently being led by the Spirit into deeper love
for the One who wrote the Word

3

The Law of Periodicity

We may assume that revivals are one of the primary methods God uses to fulfill His purposes in the world. These revivals move according to divine law. There is an orderly sequence in their movements. But can we discover this sequence? Do revivals recur at definite intervals? Can we forecast their appearance, as astronomers forecast the appearance of a comet? Obviously, this is impossible. The movements cannot be treated as an exact science. Human life does not move with precision. The wills of men and women enter, with all their inconstancy. The unexpected occurs, which changes the course of events. While these cannot stop God's plan, they may impede it.

It is impossible for us to map out with precision the recurrence of revivals. This does not mean that all that pertains to them is hidden away in the unsearchable purposes of God. It is clear that their appearance at specific times is not haphazard. One's spiritual nature is not allowed to stagnate for long periods. Neither do revivals rush upon men and women at random, without preparation or purpose. A certain law of periodicity is discernible. Even though we cannot prophesy with unerring accuracy their arrival, we can at least know that behind them is divine law and order.

An Experience from Scripture

> But the angel said to him: "Do not be afraid, Zechariah; your prayer has been heard. Your wife Elizabeth will bear you a son, and you are to call him John. He will be a joy and delight to you, and many will rejoice because of his birth."
>
> –LUKE 1:13–14

Just when hope seems lost, God shows up! Just as God's thoughts and plans are higher than ours, so also His "calendar" is often a mystery. Just as with Zechariah, revival taps into the power of prevailing prayer.

DO the WORD

- *Father God, your Word promises that when we ask according to your will, you both hear and answer. Times are desperate, but your people are not. Begin with me in a desperate cry for revival.*

A Word from Jesus

- "Then Jesus told them, 'You are going to have the light just a little while longer. Walk while you have the light, before darkness overtakes you. Whoever walks in the dark does not know where they are going'" (John 12:35).

- Sometimes our walk with the Lord seems slow and measured, but at other times, it seems fast-paced and frantic. Whatever the pace, the key is to keep walking in the light of His Word lest the darkness overtake us.

PAUSE to Encounter Jesus

- *Lord, with a sometimes dark world surrounding me, I need you and your Word as the light of my path. May your Spirit still my heart that I might often hear the whisper of your voice saying, "This is the way, walk in it" (Isaiah 30:21).*

A Cry from God's People

Though I walk in the midst of trouble, you preserve my life. You stretch out your hand against the anger of my foes; with your right hand you save me. The LORD will vindicate me; your love, LORD, endures forever—do not abandon the works of your hands.

–PSALM 138:7–8

Lord Jesus, ours is for sure a world full of 'trouble' and only you can deliver us. Please stretch forth your hand against materialism and prejudice, against division and selfish gain. Specifically, would you rid my life from _____ and revive me as the work of your hands.

Live the Word W-2:
Being a "living epistle" in reverence and awe as His Word becomes real in my life, vocation, and calling

4

The Law of Ebbing Tide

We find preceding each revival a spiritual desert. During those times, all whose hearts are alienated and are skeptical of the Church's authority break away. In those dark days unbelief reigns, while the enfeebled Church, without the strength to fight back, sits in humiliating impotence.

The Church is not blameless. The loss of hope is due to the loss of spiritual power. The loss of spiritual power is the result of leaving the heart of the Church unprotected against the world. Individually, we see this when our hearts are left in such a state. As the inner fire ceases to glow, the warmth departs. We still act like Christians. In fact, we may even look more spiritual in our effort to cover up our spiritual decay. Since the Spirit is not there, we are only offering lip service to God. The length of relapse will depend upon the character of each person. In some, because of their intense spirituality, the ebb and flow will be faint. In others, the waves will be strong and violent.

In those large movements thrown upon pages of human history, we see these facts magnified. The defection of the individual spreads until it reaches the Church. In the lowered spiritual state, corruption creeps in until, finally, the whole body is permeated with worldliness. Each generation has its own level of corruption. Thus, it would be wrong to say that revival will not occur because the corruption is not the same as previously. There is ebb and flow, but it is that of a constantly advancing tide. Yet the extent of the falling away may be great, for the fall has to be measured from the fresh advance which has been reached. Each age receives the renewed perception of God's standard of righteousness. Each age also develops its own standard of judgment. But it is according to God's standard that the Church may be condemned for defection.

An Experience from Scripture

I looked for someone among them who would build up the wall and stand before me in the gap on behalf of the land so I would not have to destroy it, but I found no one.

–Ezekiel 22:30

What a mystery this is as the Divine "partners" with us as mere humans. It's hard to imagine that He searches for us to play a role in His glorious plans.

DO the WORD

- "Here am I. Send me!" (Isaiah 6:8)

- Begin this day and each tomorrow with a yielded heart, available for "co-laboring" with Him for divine purpose!

- *Send me, Lord. This is the posture of my heart, mind, and soul. I choose you and your ways. I yield my will so that I might co-labor with you. I especially sense that you have in mind for me to join you in _____.*

A Word from Jesus

- "But you are not to be like that. Instead, the greatest among you should be like the youngest, and the one who rules like the one who serves" (Luke 22:26).

PAUSE to Encounter Jesus

- "A dispute also arose among them as to which of them was considered to be greatest" (Luke 22:24).

- Listen for the irony in the words of the "disputing disciples." Listen quietly, and you'll sense the Savior's saddened heart. Into this most vulnerable of moments, two disciples dispute over greatness! He shares of a broken body and shed blood while they strive over position. Might it not be so among us.

- *Lord, sadness is the response of my heart to the brokenness of yours. So often, your hope is for revival and things eternal while mine is bound to this world. Forgive me; cleanse me that my heart would join yours.*

A Cry from God's People

Though you have made me see troubles, many and bitter, you will restore my life again; from the depths of the earth you will again bring me up. You will increase my honor and comfort me once more.

–Psalm 71:20–21

From times of trouble to the return of revival, so are the mysteries of His ways, but it's into these mysteries that my life can declare faithfulness to the Lord.

Father God, give heed to my cry to walk faithfully with you despite surrounding troubles.

If need be, I'll walk with you and just you, no matter how others may live. Give me the testimony of revival especially in a troubled world.

Live the Word W-3:
Yielding to the Scripture's protective cautions and transforming power to bring life change in me

5

The Law of the Fullness of Time

The next fact which the study of revival discloses is that this time of spiritual deadness has its definite limits. The wave of spiritual progress recedes, but even in receding it is gathering in power and volume to return, and to rush further in. God has set a limit to the defection of His Church. When the night is at its darkest, the dawn is on the way. This next period is characterized by a dissatisfaction in many hearts. A period of gloom sets in; a weariness and exhaustion invades the heart. The pleasures of the world no longer satisfy. Thus, men and women turn to God. They realize that, in exchanging heavenly for earthly joys, they have encountered immense loss. Slowly this aching grows, the hearts of people begin to cry out to God. From a faint desire, this multiplies until it becomes a vast human need, until, in its urgency, it seems to beat at the very gates of heaven.

Within the Church, not all have fallen away. Some have mourned its loss of spiritual power and have never stopped earnestly praying for revival. Their prayer seems to go unanswered. It appears as if God has forgotten to be gracious. Gradually, the number of people praying increases. Prayer becomes more urgent and more confident. The condition of the Church becomes apparent. The need increasingly weighs upon the hearts of the devout. The longing for better things becomes an intense pain. People form into prayer groups. They do not cease imploring God to visit the souls of men and women. In many different places, unconnected with each other, this spirit of intercession awakens. With it comes an expectation that will not be denied, a premonition that there are better days ahead.

Times of awakening in the individual mostly occur at times of transition, especially from one stage of development to another. Spiritual awakenings coincide with profound change in the social or political life of the people. The value of this is apparent, since new energies are conserved and directed into channels which will lead to true progress.

The twelfth century saw Europe passing out of the Middle Ages. The feudal system was breaking up, and people were gathering in cities. A new sense of corporate life was emerging. Individuals were grouping themselves in wider combinations. Papal absolutism, which had held individuals' minds in subjection, was beginning to lose its grip. It was losing its power because of the growing independence of secular authorities and the irritation growing from newly awakened intelligence. At this time, universities began to spring up. There was a widening of sympathies, due to the Crusades and the ferment of new ideas, thus marking the close of one stage of human development and the beginning of another.

When we come to the next great movement, we stand again at a crisis in human affairs. Europe, which had in the previous period passed from childhood into youth, was in the sixteenth century passing from youth to maturity. Loyalty to the city was giving way to loyalty to the state. Europe was rearranging itself under modern geographical and national divisions. It was the time of the awakening of learning and art. Here again we see one stage of growth completed and a fresh stage beginning. After the sixteenth century, revivals shifted to the national level, since each nation differed in its stage of development. Also at this time, the Reformation had destroyed the unity and the control of Rome. Still, in these more limited movements, revival synchronizes with crises in development.

Thus, we see how at times all things seem to unite and cry out for a revival. The waters are far withdrawn and heaped up, foaming behind the barricade. The times are ripe. The soul of humankind cries out for God. A spirit of intense expectation is present. Once more the long, bitter night has ended; the dawn is at hand.

An Experience from Scripture

> Jesus spoke these things; and lifting up His eyes to heaven, He said, "Father, the hour has come; glorify Your Son, that the Son may glorify You."
>
> –JOHN 17:1

Several times over His short years of ministry, the Master had boldly declared, "My hour has NOT yet come." With this backdrop, the disciples would have taken particular note as He gazes upward and declares loudly, "THE HOUR HAS COME!"

DO the WORD

- As is often seen with the "time clock" of God, revival may come when least expected! "Come Lord Jesus; revive my heart with the cleansing and empowerment of your Spirit."

A Word from Jesus

- "As they approached the village to which they were going, Jesus continued on as if he were going farther. But they urged him strongly, 'Stay with us, for it is nearly evening; the day is almost over.' So he went in to stay with them" (Luke 24:28–29).

- This journey with the Emmaus Road disciples is filled with lessons for our walk with Him. Often unrecognized by us, He travels alongside. Unknowingly, we begin to reflect on hopes dashed and faith tested as discouragement sets in. Then we come to a fork in the road, and He awaits our invitation. Will we "urge" Him to come in or let Him pass on by?

PAUSE to Encounter Jesus

- Jesus, forever the gentleman, only enters where He is invited. But when invited, He's in charge! He takes over. He sets you at your table and takes your bread. He has you bow your head, and He blesses your food then shares your food with you!

- *Come Lord Jesus, Come! I invite you to take charge. I urge you to stay with me, remain close and reveal yourself to me. As you take over, I know I will be challenged to _____, and as I yield to you, I especially need your revelation concerning _____.*

A Cry from God's People

For your name's sake, Lord, preserve my life; in your righteousness, bring me out of trouble.

–Psalm 143:11

"For His name's sake" should become our passionate motivation. "For His name's sake" is the hope of revival. Not by works of righteousness that we have done but only by His lovingkindness will revival come.

Father, might your Name be lifted up as our only hope. We know not what to do but our eyes are upon you. Bring many across my path to inquire of my hope that I might declare, "My hope is in you, Lord!"

SPIRIT-EMPOWERED *Faith*

Live the Word W-4:
Humbly and vulnerably sharing of the Spirit's transforming work through the Word

6

The Law of the Advent of the Prophet

The next event common to the history of all great revivals is the appearance of a leader. The person sums up in himself or herself the longings of the time and interprets to the generation their innermost needs. When this person speaks, the hearers recognize his or her authority.

In this sense, the leader is recognized not as the creator but as the interpreter of the movement. The burden of the times, which others only faintly feel, becomes an intolerable load. The leader feels God's hand upon him or her and proceeds—possessed by the Holy Spirit—to be God's agent in leading men and women into new life.

Though the agent and the interpreter, the leader is not a machine. The leader brings into the movement his or her own individuality, and within certain limits defines its characteristics. When we survey the leaders in the world's revivals, we see how wide the selection is, how varied the characters of God's chosen servants. For example, Isaiah and Paul were separated by more than centuries. The same wide difference may be seen in the movements themselves because the characteristics of the movements are marked by their leaders. These characteristics were essential for the success of the movement, because each age has different needs the leader can meet.

Here the differences end. All of these great leaders share an unshakable faith in God, an overwhelming sense of a call to service, a mysterious equipment of spiritual power, and a determination to do the work of God at the expense of life itself.

An Experience from Scripture

The next day John saw Jesus coming toward him and said, "Look, the Lamb of God, who takes away the sin of the world!"

–JOHN 1:29

No better news could have been declared than this: "Behold Jesus, the Christ!" So it is in our day;

people whether they realize it or not are longing to see Jesus. Their hope of Jesus is often found in us—His people—as we live out His Word.

DO the WORD

- The first-century revival of following Jesus was empowered as people took note that His followers "had been with Jesus" (Acts 4:13).

- *This is the hope of our day, and it is me to whom the world is looking. Lord, may it be found true that others observe in my life the marks of intimacy with Jesus.*

A Word from Jesus

- "As you sent me into the world, I have sent them into the world" (John 17:18).

- Imagine the wonder and privilege of "being sent" by the Creator for divine purpose, and the further wonder that you have been sent in the manner and power of Jesus.

PAUSE to Encounter Jesus

- Pause with a yielded heart and say yes to being sent by the Lord; claim the promise that He goes with you. Celebrate that you are on a divine mission with eternal significance.

- *Lord Jesus, I'm humbled to be sent as your ambassador; I'm grateful you go with me. May those around me notice you.*

A Cry from God's People

See how I love your precepts; preserve my life, LORD, in accordance with your love. All your words are true; all your righteous laws are eternal.

–PSALM 119:159–160

Love of His Word is a mark of revival, and that which we truly love, we make a priority. Scripture speaks of five avenues through which we encounter His Word: hearing, reading, studying, memorizing, and meditating. Have I moved beyond simply "hearing" the Word in various meetings to embrace more personal encounters of reading and study? Have memorization and meditation of the Word become my common practice?

Lord, revive in me a passionate love for your Word that it might take priority in my life and schedule.

Live the Word W-5:
Meditating consistently on more and more of the Word hidden in the heart

7

The Law
of Awakening

When these elements of preparation, timing, and leadership fall into place, the awakening occurs. The people that walked in darkness see a great light. They fling off the garments of despair and celebrate life.

In each movement there is something incalculable. New forces, long preparing under the surface, burst into being. The revival's tide rolls on from an unseen continent and moves with a fathering, unresisting momentum. Yet while each is individual, there is uniformity. Each revival is characterized by the extraordinary swiftness with which it spreads. Once the first words of the new message are spoken, mysterious forces arise, like the wind, and carry them from place to place. The revival spreads like an epidemic. It bursts out in places that have not been in contact with other infected places, and individuals are moved in multitudes. Luther's nailing of the 95 Theses on the church door at Wittenberg seemed to be of little importance, but it was a spark to a dry forest, and the fire that it began has yet to be put out. When Wesley stood up in the open air to address a crowd of illiterate miners, no one knew that it would be the beginning of one of the largest Protestant churches in the world. The rapidity with which revivals spread is an indication of the silent preparation which goes on beneath the surface long before the revival itself takes place. It shows how God's Spirit is always active.

Everyone who studies the phenomena of revivals is struck by the similarity of the effects produced upon those who are touched by them. Two of these stand out with startling vividness and are common to all.

First of all, is the deep conviction of sin. In the intense spiritual light, the sin and guilt of the awakened soul stand out in terrifying blackness. Not only are their sins laid bare, but the convicted see themselves as in a mirror. Every sin, seemingly minor, confronts them. Their sin drags them to judgment. Terror seizes them as the conviction of sin burns like fire. Yet this terror of the Lord is not the terror of punishment. It is inspired by a sense of having rebelled against God. Under this agony of conviction, men and women openly confess their sins. Their one intense longing is to cast their sins forever from them, to be brought into reconciliation and peace with God. Even those who are only attracted by curiosity feel the irresistible power dragging them to confession. Some, though totally ignorant of spiritual things, are brought to conversion.

The dulled conscience has permitted many things to creep within the Church's doors. They might not be wrong in themselves, but lend to dull the edge of its spiritual life. When the inner fires cease to glow with love for Christ, there is nothing left to defend the Church from the world. In many cases, divisions arise or worship is reduced to cold formalities. Worldly practices are permitted in order to maintain interest. Although they are condemned by many, there is not the power to eject them. The Church becomes worldly, selfish, and almost Christless.

With a revival, all this is changed. The Church's long defection ends. A new consciousness of sin is awakened in the Church as well as in the individual. There passes over the Church a wave of deep conviction and shame. Then follows a time of reformation, of purging the impurities. It seeks by united prayer and intense zeal to bring to Jesus those who do not know Him. This reformation of the Church is not sudden. The Church absorbs those large masses affected by the revival, and fresh life is poured back into the hearts of its members. Actually, the fresh winds of revival may break outside the boundary or walls of the organized church and become the spiritual fire to ignite the church and the divine detergent to cleanse and refresh its ministry.

The second characteristic produced by a revival movement is joy. When the night is passed, and with it the agony of conviction and the grief and terror of sin, there breaks upon the humbled heart the peace of forgiveness. No joy on earth compares with this that awakens in the forgiven heart. People have exhausted language in trying to describe it.

At such times, Isaiah's description of the mountains and hills breaking forth into singing and all the trees of the field clapping their hands does not appear excessive. To those caught in the revival's flood, all the world seems changed. Their hearts are light, and their faces glow.

This joy is not limited to those newly converted. It fills the hearts of those who are already followers of Christ. It sweeps into the Church, making all its worship pulse and glow with spiritual fervor.

This is the effect of revival, wherever it appears. It leaves in its wake numberless men and women whose faces glow with a new light and whose hearts throb with an intense and pure joy.

This new gladness characteristically finds an outlet in song. Song is the natural expression of the jubilant heart. It is the escape valve for feelings which are too exhilarating to remain silent. Most of the great leaders of revival have been poets, and the revival is born along the wings of praise. Singing has been a prominent feature in most revivals.

The conditions for revival are timeless. There are no twenty-first-century shortcuts. In 1904, all Wales was aflame with revival. The nation had drifted far from God, and spiritual conditions were at their lowest. Church attendance was pitiably poor and practices of immorality and sinful indulgence abounded on every hand. Suddenly, through the power of prayer, like an unexpected tornado, the power of God moved in and swept over the land. Churches were crowded with three services every day lasting from 10 a.m. to 12 midnight. Evan Roberts was the human instrument God used to turn the tide of revival.

There was little preaching—mostly singing, testimonies, and prayer. There were no hymnbooks, no offerings, no advertising—but everybody sang. History records there were more songs composed than sermons delivered. Nothing had ever come over Wales with such mighty, far-reaching results.

Infidels were converted. Drunks, thieves, and thugs by the hundreds were born again. Multitudes of the most respected and socially prominent were converted. Old debts were paid, theaters and pubs closed, and the mules in the mines refused to work, being unused to the transformed attitudes of the workers, nor were they thereafter required to work on the Lord's Day.

Whatever the expression, the gladness itself is never absent. In many, it becomes so extreme that it can be dangerous. Almost every revival is accompanied by outbursts of excitement and by startling physical phenomena. Outbreaks of physical anguish are followed by outbursts of uncontrollable joy. The effect of these extreme emotions on unstable people is often disastrous. A revival's value is not to be based on these exceptions. Many who are looking for reasons to point a finger at the movement use these cases to justify their criticisms. Those whose minds are fixed on the trivial and whose hearts are void of spiritual life miss the true impact of the revival on the individual soul.

All revivals affect large masses of the community. They leave a permanent influence for good behind them and create a new era in progress. All revivals start from the bottom. Their leaders are almost entirely of the people. Their greatest influence is on the poor and upon those neglected by the Church. When faith is waning, the Church loses its spirit of sacrifice. It becomes self-seeking. It uses its influence over its members to obtain comfort and ease. As a consequence, those masses of the community who are unattractive because of their ignorance or poverty are neglected.

When the news of redeeming love is proclaimed with passionate joy and conviction, the poor are reached. It is the common people who hear it with gladness. They live in poverty, neglected and uncared for by those who ought to give their lives for them. Having found little to satisfy their hunger for love, their hearts are drawn to the message of God's love. Drawn into Christianity, their hearts are uplifted by pure emotion. Their whole lives are changed, and they become an asset to the wealth of a nation. Thus a revival means the recreation of large portions of the community, a segment that once seemed to be a deficit to society. In the light of this fact, it would be trite to say that the next revival will be an ethical one. All revivals are ethical. They move, if authentic and sent from above, not merely in the realm of emotion but in the sphere of the conscience and the will. They leave behind them not merely joyful, but changed, lives. The chains of addiction are broken. Revivals implant a new set of emotions within the heart. They inspire men and women to develop their characters and enrich their lives through education, self-discipline, and especially prayer.

The effect of a revival upon the Church is no less profound and far-reaching. For while the word *revive* literally means "to bring to life again," the word in its religious context includes the awakening of those who were dead and rejuvenating those who were alive but slumbering.

Every revival exposes the spiritual decay of the Church, with its worldliness and hypocrisy. This spiritual decay seems to move along two different lines.

The first tendency is for the doctrine of the Church to lose its power to convict the conscience, convince the mind, or move the mind. After a time of immense theological interest, that interest begins to wane. People's minds are attracted by fresh discoveries in other fields. Thus, theology fails to keep pace with the fresh thought of the age. It is outdated and treated with contempt by other areas of human thought, which are on the cutting edge of progress.

In addition, each age requires a restatement of truth. The truth does not change, but our comprehension of it does. We are taught to see it from new angles and with an altered perspective. Thus, there is the necessity for a new statement, for a reinterpretation of the old words in terms of the new. For words are like coins, of full value fresh from the mint, but capable of being defaced and robbed of their full value. In spiritually dead times, preachers continue to use the old words. Once so full of power, now they have no impact. This is partly because the language has changed, but also because the words have become the mere jargon of the pulpit. Preachers mumble out their clichés that have no impact on the conscience or the heart, because they themselves have ceased to be moved by them.

The Church passes through a period of skepticism. Unbelief chills its vital fires, and hypocrisy leaves its message powerless.

With the first pronouncement of the leader's living message, all this passes away. A new aspect of truth is declared, or an old and forgotten truth is restated, and suddenly people's hunger is appeased. They are fed again with the bread of life.

The second tendency in spiritual decay is for worship to become formal. The pulpit exalts ritual until the spirit is crushed. Religion is represented, not as a response of the soul to God, but as a rigid performance of outward observances and ceremonies. Ritual forms of worship, even when elaborate, are not evil in themselves. Some people find their spiritual life enriched by them. They are not dangerous to the general worshiper as long as the spiritual life of the church is intense and the form is the expression of the spirit. It is when the spiritual fire departs that the danger appears. The form then becomes an end in itself. Strict obedience to it becomes religion and is coldly offered to God in lieu of spiritual worship. At such times, outward observance increases rather than diminishes. The self-righteous are given opportunity to display their zeal, while they impose heavy burdens upon the hearts of the humble and the ignorant. This shift of focus, from inner life to outward observance, divorces religion from morality.

At such a time, the pastorate degenerates. The love of wealth, ease, and power appears. Ministers become the object of scorn to the skeptical and indifferent.

An example of this is the condition of Israel at the time of Christ. When the Israelites returned from the captivity, the rulers of the people turned to the Law with passionate devotion. While this devotion remained, the spiritual life of Israel was maintained. No sooner did it diminish than the minute observances of the Law became intolerable bondage. Their religion, emptied of its spiritual content, became a worship of externals. So bankrupt of spiritual discernment did the people become that the hypocrite became the popular ideal of the religious person. They had become so dead that they not only failed to recognize the Messiah but crucified Him as a heretic.

Christ had lamented over such people—"O Jerusalem, Jerusalem, the one who kills the prophets and stones those who are sent to her! How often I wanted to gather your children together, as a hen gathers her chicks under her wings, but you were not willing!" (Matthew 23:37 NKJV).

This despiritualizing of religion, this worship of the form rather than of the spirit, is a constant threat to the Church. However, the moment the first breath of revival touches the heart of the Church, the chains which bind it are broken. With a new joy, it returns to simplicity of worship and intense sincerity of life.

An Experience from Scripture

He has shown you, O mortal, what is good.
And what does the LORD require of you?
To act justly and to love mercy and to walk
humbly with your God.

–MICAH 6:8

Many would view this succinct truth as the cornerstone of the Old Testament. Priority is given to living a humble life "vertically" with our God, and a life of justice and kindness "horizontally" toward others. In a similar way, it was said of Jesus that He simply went about "doing good" (Acts 10:38). In our complex, high-tech world, maybe an important lesson we should see is the value of "simplicity and purity of our devotion to Christ" (2 Corinthians 11:3).

DO the WORD

- *Father, our hearts are burdened that we have at times been led astray from the purity of our devotion to you and the simplicity of our love of others. Revive in me humility, justice, and kindness that I might be known as one who goes about doing good.*

A Word from Jesus

- "I am coming to you now, but I say these things while I am still in the world, so that they may have the full measure of my joy within them" (John 17:13).

- Consider this One who "ever lives to make intercession," our great High Priest. We listen in on His prayer, and He speaks your name. You lean in even closer, and hear the words, "My joy be made full."

PAUSE to Encounter Jesus

- *Jesus, flood my life with a joy which is not of this world. By your Spirit, fill me with joy not found in what I acquire, accomplish, or achieve, but rooted in the truth that I am your beloved! Though I have not seen you, I love you and experience joy inexpressible and full of glory.* (See 1 Peter 1:8)

A Cry from God's People

I will show the holiness of my great name, which has been profaned among the nations, the name you have profaned among them. Then the nations will know that I am the LORD, declares the Sovereign LORD, when I am proved holy through you before their eyes.

–EZEKIEL 36:23

When will the Lord show Himself strong in our day? When will the nations know that He is the Lord? The answer becomes personal: "When He proves Himself holy in me!"

Father, I yield to your perfecting work; transform me by your Spirit that I might reflect Christ.

Live the Word W-6:
Encountering Jesus in the Word for deepened transformation in Christ-likeness

8

The Law
of Variety

The appearance of revivals owes nothing to chance; they are a witness to God's sovereignty. Used of God for the progress of the world, they revitalize men's and women's lives. They appear at intervals and at points of crisis in individuals' lives. Although these cannot be delineated with precision, we are able to see a regularity in their appearance and, within certain limits, to anticipate their coming. Next, we see that there is sufficient data to conclude that the laws which govern them are constant, like any other of God's laws. First of all, we perceive that they come when preparations have been made, when the times are ripe. Next, their appearance is signaled by certain infallible signs, one of which is a growing discontentment in individuals' hearts with corruption and back-sliding. With this comes an intense craving for something better. A growing spirit of expectation that change is coming soon develops. At last, when contributing streams converge at a definite point, there suddenly appears the messenger who speaks for God and whose voice people instantly recognize and obey.

Another similarity is what occurs when the revival movement is set in motion. When the voice of the leader is heard, vast forces, which seem to have been lying dormant, are awakened. The revival spreads like fire, and huge numbers of people are affected. Wherever it goes, and into whatever heart it enters, it creates an overwhelming realization of sin—then confession. With the forgiveness of sin comes a joy that expresses itself in song. The main effect of the revival is felt in the inner life. It awakens new spiritual emotions. It sharpens lives into subjection to the will of God. It brings the Church back to simplicity, sincerity, and a renewed spiritual vitality.

As in all of God's dealings with His creation, there are the elements of the mysterious. No two revivals are identical. While possessing common elements, every expression of each law contains unique characteristics. Each is adapted to the need of the times. It is modified first by the conditions of the age, secondly by nationality, and then by the individual characteristics of its leader. This outward variety is a necessity for success. Were all revivals identical, the majority of the people would remain unaffected. Variety is a source of life.

A revival which affects one nation or people may have little influence upon another. In many cases where the attempt was made to duplicate a revival's characteristics, the attempt not only failed but also stirred up irritation and strife.

An illustration of this fact may be discovered in the history of the Reformation in the sixteenth century. That movement, which profoundly affected the Teutonic races, left the Latin races almost unaffected. Its geographical area was so pronounced that it still remains, and the chasm which it created still separates the Roman Catholics from the Protestants.

Another fact about revival movements is the variety in the character of their appeal. Sometimes that appeal moves in the realm of the affection. Emotional revivals are, of all revivals, the most immediately effective and the least enduring.

Sometimes a revival's chief characteristic is theological, emerging in the discovery of some new truth. Each adapts itself to the urgent need of the age, and thus produces the most permanent results. Each wins its way because of its adaptation to the needs of the times and to the temperament of the people. What is effective for one cannot be effective for all.

One other significant fact regarding the variety in revivals is that movement in one direction is often followed by a movement in an opposite one. In religion, as in politics, there are two distinct camps, liberal and conservative. The watchword of the one is Freedom—that of the other is Authority. The conflict between the two is constant, but each represents too deep a factor of human life to destroy the other. Thus, a revival which carries to one extreme will be followed by a countermovement in the other direction.

Striking as the similar points are in revivals, there are also as many illustrations of variety. The same laws are in each, but as with all the laws of God, there is adaptation and readjustment.

———

An Experience from Scripture

Flesh gives birth to flesh, but the Spirit gives birth to spirit.

–John 3:6

Ideas, plans, and decisions that have been birthed "in the flesh" will ever remain flesh; it's vanity to beseech God to bless that which He did not originate, but herein, we find hope and promise!

His Spirit is longing to birth and empower His ways in us, bringing freshness and revival.

DO the WORD

- *Lord Jesus, I turn away from my own initiative to wait on you; I yield to the initiative of Your Spirit to bring forth your thoughts, plans, and ways. "Birth" in and through me those things new and eternal.*

A Word from Jesus

- "Neither do people pour new wine into old wineskins. If they do, the skins will burst; the wine will run out and the wineskins will be ruined. No, they pour new wine into new wineskins, and both are preserved" (Matthew 9:17).

- The freshness of where the Spirit blows reshapes our traditions and methods. The gospel message would forever reshape temple worship. Holding onto old "wine skins" rather than embracing His fresh work brings irrelevance.

PAUSE to Encounter Jesus

- *Jesus, I yield to the freshness of what you desire to do, confident that methods and traditions will be reshaped according to your will. I release any hold on the "old" in order for you to do a "new" thing in and through my life.*

A Cry from God's People

Then you will call on me and come and pray to me, and I will listen to you. You will seek me and find me when you seek me with all your heart.

–JEREMIAH 29:12–13

It's a certain truth that if you don't feel close to God, guess who moved? He remains the same, available, and approachable.

Father, I acknowledge that I have turned aside from other things to seek you, to pray, and to believe you will hear and answer. My confident trust is in you, Lord. I especially seek you over _____.

Live the Word W-7:
A life-explained as one of "experiencing Scripture"

9

The Law
of Recoil

Every revival has a time limit. It has its day, then it recedes. Luther set the limit to a revival at thirty years, Isaac Taylor at fifty. Rarely does it last beyond a generation. But in duration, two revivals are rarely alike. Because of the variables and their different characters, the extent and duration are varied. The constant factor is that, whatever the size of the wave, it has its limits marked out for it.

Many people are swept into a revival's current by yielding to emotion while their natures remain unchanged. They cool down and are swept back into the world again. Nothing can be said about the percentage who fall away. Revival movements differ in this also. In revivals where emotions are

held in check and the appeal is made to the conscience, the effect is more permanent.

The good effect of a revival runs on long after
the surprise and emotion are gone. Yet there comes
a time when this seems to end, and the movement
falls into decay. It becomes not an influence for
good but for evil. Instead of liberating, it becomes
an agent of oppression. Few things in life are more
pathetic than how quickly the good gets tarnished
or corrupted. Such was the case with the recoil that
came after the days of Luther, with its bitterness
and rivalries.

In all revival movements, this law of recoil
must be recognized in order to be wisely and
prayerfully anticipated. A wider knowledge of
such movements will prepare the Church for this,
and thus its dangers can be minimized. It is the
ebb of the wave which falls back, only to gain
strength to push further on. When each revival
has made its original contribution to the wealth
of human experience, it falls back to give place
to something else. There is no need to mourn.
As Tennyson truthfully said, "The old order
changeth, yielding place to new, and God ful-
fills Himself in many ways, lest one good custom
should corrupt the world."[*]

---

[*]   Alfred Lord Tennyson, poem "Morte d'Arthur."

This longing for a fresh movement from God was expressed most succinctly by the psalmist: "Oh, revive us! Then your people can rejoice in you again" (Psalm 85:6 TLB). We echo that longing when we read of past revivals, then fall to our knees and cry, "Do it again, Lord. Do it again!"

An Experience from Scripture

The poor will see and be glad—you who seek God, may your hearts live! The LORD hears the needy and does not despise his captive people.

–PSALM 69:32–33

Very few times do we hear Jesus describe Himself, but one of those key words He uses is "humble." "Take my yoke upon you and learn of me, for I am humble and gentle" (Matthew 11:28–30). A humble heart is one that experiences revival and a supernatural life.

DO the WORD

- Meditate quietly on Christ in His side of the yoke as He invites you to come and take the other side. The Master Teacher will mentor you in humility and gentleness.

- *Lord Jesus, I see myself now yoked with you; I want to learn of you. You've often loved others around me, without me—but no more! In humility, I join you to co-labor with you for your kingdom's sake.*

A Word from Jesus

- "One of them, when he saw he was healed, came back, praising God in a loud voice. He threw himself at Jesus' feet and thanked him—and he was a Samaritan. Jesus asked, 'Were not all ten cleansed? Where are the other nine? Has no one returned to give praise to God except this foreigner?'" (Luke 17:15–18)

- "Where are the other nine?" With these few words, we sense the sorrowed heart of the Savior. He is not asking, "Does anyone know where the other nine lepers are?" His question is personal and pain-filled. "Why are they not here before me offering thanks?"

PAUSE to Encounter Jesus

- Christ's acquaintance with sorrow and grief was more than just at Calvary. Often in His humanity, He would experience rejection, loneliness, and ungratefulness. Quietly consider all that He's done for you, and then imagine yourself joining the one leper giving Him thanks.

- *Lord Jesus, for all you are to me and all you've done, I give you thanks. As you receive the praise of grateful saints, may you NEVER look around and I'm nowhere in sight. I long to be one of the faithful and grateful who regularly give you glory.*

A Cry from God's People

Then, at the evening sacrifice, I rose from my self-abasement, with my tunic and cloak torn, and fell on my knees with my hands spread out to the LORD my God and prayed: "I am too ashamed and disgraced, my God, to lift up my face to you, because our sins are higher than our heads and our guilt has reached to the heavens."

–EZRA 9:5–6

Lord I'm ashamed that I have settled for the things of this world; I've lost the expectancy of the miraculous. Forgive me. Cleanse me. Strengthen my faith in the works of your Spirit. Create in me a clean heart, O God, that I might serve you and your plans for our world.

Live the Word W-8:
Living "naturally supernatural" in all of life as His Spirit makes the written Word (*logos*) the living Word (*Rhema*)

10

The Law of
the Theology
of Revivals

I t is important for us to know the great doctrines
that have awakened people to new life in past
centuries.

First of all, we see that all revivals fall back
upon simplicity. They cut through the accumu-
lated doctrines and subtle complexities until they
arrive at some aspect of truth which has become
forgotten or has been buried by tradition. In
perspective, every revival goes back to apostolic
times and to the spirit of the early Church. Each
attempts to strip the Church and the individual
of the heavy burdens imposed in a time of decay,
a time when men and women are more intent on

proving the doctrines of the Church than on living them. Its central effort is to get back to the source of life.

When we analyze the messages in those great days of revival, we see one message which is never absent, a message which is at the heart of every movement. This is the message of the Cross.

How much we need the focus of the apostle Paul: "But God forbid that I should glory except in the cross of our Lord Jesus Christ, by whom the world has been crucified to me, and I to the world" (Galatians 6:14 NKJV). In every case where the life of the Church has become powerless, it will be found that the message of the Cross has either been denied or forgotten.

If this is true, and it is, then its value is of the utmost importance. It shows that, whenever men's and women's hearts are profoundly moved, they turn to the Cross for satisfaction, with the same instinct with which a child in need turns to its mother. Redeeming love is the message underlying every great spiritual movement of the Church. Never has there been a spiritual movement in the Christian Church in which Christ has not been realized as the source of life. Every revival is a return to Christ. Each comes from a fresh recognition of His power to save.

In the time of the Reformation, the doctrine of

justification by faith had ceased to exist. Ecclesias-ticism so dominated people's minds that they were blind to the truth when reading Paul's epistles. This is a curious fact about the human mind, that it has the power only to see what agrees with cur-rent opinion. Every age is imprisoned in its own conceptions and has to be set free by the minds which refuse to be enslaved.

There is a vast difference in the ways people hold the same doctrines. They are held either as supreme or as of secondary importance. It makes all the difference in the life of the Church when prominence is given to the essential doctrines. The Church is revived when it is brought back to Christ, when it takes up the Cross again. With the message of salvation burning in its heart, it goes out once again as its Master did "to seek and to save them that are lost."

Also, it is a significant fact that no religious system which rejects the Cross knows anything of revivals in the same way that Christianity does. Their ranks are recruited from those who become skeptical in the days of depression. They are never flooded with enthusiastic life, nor charged with messages which move large amounts of people to the knowledge of divine things.

An Experience from Scripture

"You are a king, then!" said Pilate. Jesus
answered, "You say that I am a king. In fact,
the reason I was born and came into the
world is to testify to the truth. Everyone
on the side of truth listens to me." "What
is truth?" retorted Pilate. With this he went
out again to the Jews gathered there and
said, "I find no basis for a charge against
him."

–JOHN 18:37–38

What a shock this must have been for Pilate.
Truth is a Person, standing before him! Jesus
makes truth personal, relational, and by His Spirit
truth is made alive in us.

DO the WORD

- *Lord as I reflect on the revival of Pentecost,
  I'm reminded of the power of God's people
  doing God's book. As your Spirit was poured
  out on all flesh, inquiry was made, and Peter's
  response was that "THIS you are experiencing
  is simply THAT written in Scripture" (Acts
  2:16). Give my life this testimony that others
  would see me and see truth.*

A Word from Jesus

- "Jesus answered: 'Don't you know me, Philip, even after I have been among you such a long time? Anyone who has seen me has seen the Father. How can you say, 'Show us the Father'?" (John 14:9).

- Again, we sense the Savior's sorrow that those nearest Him really don't know Him. How tragic and challenging that I might have known about Him but not really known Him!

PAUSE to Encounter Jesus

- *Jesus, it's all about you, and my prayer is that I would pursue intimacy with you, never satisfied to merely know "about you."*

A Cry from God's People

Also, seek the peace and prosperity of the city to which I have carried you into exile. Pray to the LORD for it, because if it prospers, you too will prosper.

—JEREMIAH 29:7

Pause to invite God's healing and help in your city. Next, declare your availability to engage as He might direct. Begin with prayer for your city and trust the leadership of His Spirit to give direction.

Father God, I celebrate your burden for my city as you see them as sheep without a shepherd, suffering much under the pain of their own choices. Engage me as your co-laborer to see your glory made known and your name exalted.

Live the Word W-9:
Living abundantly "in the present" as His Word brings healing to hurt and anger, guilt, fear and condemnation—which are heart hindrances to life abundant

11

The Law of the Coming Movement

Let us close with a glance into the future. With the help of these stated biblical principles, we will ask what the future has in store. Before we can do this, we must first examine the present condition of the Church and read the signs of our times.

First of all, no one pretends that all is well with the Church today. When allowance is made for exaggeration, there are enough problems left to arouse deep soul searching. On every side, there is complaint of the Church's loss of spiritual power, the increasing indifference of its people, and a decrease in membership. Where there is not decline, there is a conscious arrest of her influence, and in the world a hostility to her claims.

The Church is still active. Never was there more activity and less result. There is abundant energy, but it is not conquering energy conscious of its power, but feverish energy, conscious of its impotence. The message of the pulpit has largely lost its power to convince, and the preacher, his power to lead to conversion.

When we look beneath the surface, we see much to account for this. We have been passing through an age of commercialism. Never in the history of the world have the hearts of individuals been set with such a passion upon materialism. This has deadened men's and women's hearts to the Gospel. But this is not the sole reason. The Church itself has not escaped from materialism's corruption. It has been allowed to creep in and devitalize the Church's spiritual witness.

A new conscience is arising which is judging the Church by new standards. People are growing conscious of a contradiction between Christ's attitude toward the poor and the attitude of those who profess to be Christians. There is a growing sense of social injustice. Indignation is rising because, in the presence of this, the Church has remained silent—ignoring those who need it the most.

Much of this accusation is undeserved and can be repudiated by individual congregations. But concerning the Church in general, it is impossible to deny it. Because of this, many are making sacrificial efforts to rectify their attitudes, though they know that the Church is not behind them.

Another reason for the present state of impotence arises because we have gone through an age of theological unrest. Our foundations are shifting. It is an age of transition, and such periods are ones of suffering. This unrest in the area of belief has arisen through the scientific revival which has characterized this century. The progress has been amazing. But no area of human thought has been more threatened than theology. The theory of evolution has challenged the whole Christian creed and has demanded a reevaluation of its essential beliefs. Historic research dealing with the Bible has left nothing unexamined which was once considered too holy to touch.

For many, the result of these changes has been the unsettlement of belief; for others, the loss of their faith. For all, an uncertainty regarding even the most central doctrines has arisen. These changes have introduced into the pulpit an insecurity brought about by preachers who were not quite certain of their ground. A tendency to leave many of the disputed doctrines alone and rely upon moral precepts and good living has arisen.

The result is that much, if not all, of the message of Christianity has been silenced. Passion is simulated. Energy is directed toward useless things. People in the pew are unconsciously affected by the absence of certainty and of intense conviction. So pulpit and pew are united in a common misgiving. People find it easy to drift from the Church. Their consciences are unaffected by their relapse, because there is not the atmosphere of reality which makes neglecting the Church a sin.

If this is true, then it is a fact which should awaken the dullest heart concerned about the welfare of the world and his or her own spiritual life. Of course, a weakening Church means that the forces working against the Church are growing stronger. It makes us turn to the future and ask, "What is before us? Is the day of the Church over? Must we live on to see the decline, until it results in death?"

From such questions we can turn away with a smile. The Church is not on the eve of destruction. It is on the eve of a revival. Like the day that comes when the long night is over, so every revival comes after times of tribulation. Nothing in the world is more certain than this. The question is not if, but when. Regarding such a question, it would be impious to speak with authority. It is not for us to know the times which God has hidden. At the same time, there is much to give us hope.

When we turn to the present social and political conditions, it is not difficult to see that a great revolution is taking place. There is emerging a multitude of the neglected, demanding recognition, justice, and human rights. A new cry is heard today. The cry not only pierces the halls of government, but echoes like a wail in our churches. It is the cry of those who are awakening to a sense of bitter wrong and of social discontent. As crude as their cry may be, it is valid. People are coming to the recognition that the poor and deprived are men and women made in the image of God, thus having value.

All awakenings are dangerous if unattended by spiritual illumination and allowed to grow in hostility to religion. As a rule, today's leaders are often not found in the Church. They are standing outside the Church, accusing it of betraying God. Whether this is true or not is irrelevant, only this pathetic and humiliating fact of history has to be recalled: nearly every great revival has originated outside of the Church. This may not happen today, but in times of degeneracy, the Spirit of Christ is often found outside of the Church. Again, when the Spirit is freshly poured out, it is not the Church, but those outside it who make the first response. Only afterward is the Church awakened.

The Church today appears helpless to cope with its growing responsibilities. The problems are so great that the Church seems to sink under the weight of them. It is the Church's duty, not to solve the problems, but to give an inspiration. It is a flood of new spiritual life that is needed. When the heart is alive, the hardest problem becomes solvable. Love awakes and finds its own channels. It is the Church's coldness that makes problems unsolvable.

The solution is a revival of spiritual religion—a new breath which will pass over the valley of dry bones and make them live. The world is ready for this revival, whether or not the Church is. For the Church, revival means humiliation, a bitter knowledge of unworthiness, and an open and humiliating confession of sin. It comes to scorch before it heals.

This is why revival has been unpopular with many within the Church. It says nothing to them of the power they have learned to love, the ease, or success. It accuses them of sin; it tells them that they are dead. It calls them to forsake all else and follow Christ.

Is the Church today ready to hear that voice? Some doubt it. It is upon the hearts of the few that the agony falls. Revivals are not preceded by the Church becoming aware of the need, but by a few people here and there, who, feeling the need, begin to entreat God for a revival. This sense of need grows into a burden, until the cry becomes an agony. This is the cry which God cannot deny.

No revival can come from below. All attempts to create a revival fail. Nor can we bring a revival down, since prayer is not the cause of a revival, but the human preparation for one. By prayer we prepare the soil.

Is there a disposition to pray for revival? Are devout men and women everywhere becoming alarmed, not for the success of the Church, but for the glory of Christ? If not, then the night is not far spent, a deeper darkness is yet to come. For what use would a revival be if we were not prepared for it? It would pass over us without doing its work. J. Hudson Taylor affirmed this when he wrote, "The spirit of prayer is, in essence, the spirit of revival."[*]

But there are signs that this burden to pray is being laid upon the souls of men and women. Many are beginning to passionately long for better things and to agonize in prayer. To fail in this is to be a traitor to Christ and to the deepest need of the world around us.

Encouragement that the dawn is near comes

---

[*] J. Hudson Taylor, as quoted by Bob Griffin, *Firestorms of Revival* (Lake Mary, FL: Creation House, 2006), 73.

from another side. Some have pointed out that we have been passing through an age of criticism, when much of the accepted truth has not been able to stand the test. Most careful onlookers are convinced that the worst is over. The destructive era has ended and the constructive era has begun. A great change has overcome the leaders of science and of thought. There is a new reverence for the spiritual life, and thought has drifted far from the agnostic position.

One of the most significant facts connected with this new movement is the orthodox position. Much has changed, but nothing vital in Christian belief has been lost. The old lives still in the new. With the recognition of the spiritual reality, it is possible to return to that same sense of security of belief which makes a revival of religion possible. As long as belief was uncertain and those responsible to defend the Church's faith were panic-stricken, this was impossible. With the new confidence, there is also arising a longing for a revived Church.

It is encouraging that this dryness is only local. In other parts of the world, the wave that is subsiding here is flowing in full force. In Asia, Latin America, and Africa, Christianity is spreading rapidly. But not only there is Christianity growing, but also in Eastern Europe the growth is remarkable.

Of what character will the next revival be? No

one can say, but there are certain things that we can hope for; others we may regard with certainty. First of all, no revival would be worth anything if it excluded those who are alienated from the Church. Whatever the message is, it must bring the people back to their heritage within the Church. It must bring the Church back to the needs of the poor and underprivileged and disenfranchised. Such a message will demand a greater sacrifice than the Church has been called to make since its birth. For it was not power and position which won the hearts of the poor and outcast in those days, but it was the Church's poverty and love.

The next revival will move us toward unity, which goes along with the spirit of our age. Denominationalism is breaking down around us. In the face of the complexities of modern life, the cry for unity is heard. All that is needed is the increase of love that comes with revival, to cement those unions already formed.

Whatever form the coming awakening may take, we may be certain that it will bring us back to the essentials. This is the result of every true revival. It cuts through the trappings until it gets to the core of life. It leads men and women back to simplicity. When the heart earnestly seeks God, it takes the shortest route. Above all, it will bring us back to Christ.

The day may be near. Even now He may be preparing His messenger.

"But who can endure the day of His coming? And who can stand when He appears? For He is like a refiner's fire and like launderers' soap. He will sit as a refiner and a purifier of silver; He will purify the sons of Levi, and purge them as gold and silver, that they may offer to the LORD an offering in righteousness. Then the offering of Judah and Jerusalem will be pleasant to the LORD, as in the days of old, as in former years. And I will come near you for judgment; I will be a swift witness against sorcerers, against adulterers, against perjurers, against those who exploit wage earners and widows and orphans, and against those who turn away an alien—because they do not fear Me," says the LORD of hosts. ... "But to you who fear My name the Sun of Righteousness shall arise with healing in His wings; and you shall go out and grow fat like stall-fed calves." (Malachi 3:2–5; 4:2 NKJV)

An Experience from Scripture

At that time his voice shook the earth, but now he has promised, "Once more I will shake not only the earth but also the heavens." The words "once more" indicate the removing of what can be shaken—that is, created things—so that what cannot be shaken may remain.

–HEBREWS 12:26–27

Man-made things being shaken … such is the testimony of our day. Quietly listen, and you'll hear the crumbling sounds of irrelevant religion. Listen again, and you'll sense His calling to join Him in "those things that cannot be shaken."

DO the WORD

- *Father, I want to be a part of your witness to eternal things. As man-made things crumble, many will look for the real and genuine. By your Spirit, make those qualities a reality in my life.*

A Word from Jesus

- "The King will reply, 'Truly I tell you, whatever you did for one of the least of these brothers and sisters of mine, you did for me'" (Matthew 25:40).

- "Whatever you did for one of the least of these!" What a shocking declaration this is from the Savior, and what a challenge to you and me. Intentionality is required as most do not live among the least. Humility is essential, and compassion is the motivation.

PAUSE to Encounter Jesus

- *Jesus, I long to join you in loving the least of these well! Grant me wisdom in how and where; plus, empower me by your Spirit not to miss the opportunities you present to me.*

A Cry from God's People

My prayer is not for them alone. I pray also for those who will believe in me through their message, that all of them may be one, Father, just as you are in me and I am in you. May they also be in us so that the world may believe that you have sent me.

–John 17:20-21

The testimony of unity is unmistakable and not easily ignored. Thus, the enemy, at all costs, strives to divide and distract. Pause to ask for the supernatural witness of oneness among His people (see Romans 15:7; John 13:34).

Heavenly Father, remove from my life division, judgment, and prejudice. Grant me your supernatural grace to accept as I've been accepted and love as I have been loved.

 Live the Word W-10:
Implicit, unwavering trust that His Word will never fail

Acknowledgments

Our deepest thanks to the Great Commandment Network, David Ferguson, and Terri Snead for their partnership in the Spirit-Empowered Faith exercises written for *Revival Now: A Jesus Awakening*. We would also like to extend our appreciation to Alisa Johnson, Kathy Maas, Ralph Williams, and Emily Adams for their assistance in the preparation of this booklet.

Appendix 1

ABOUT THE GREAT COMMANDMENT NETWORK

The Great Commandment Network is an international collaborative network of strategic kingdom leaders from the faith community, marketplace, education, and caregiving fields who prioritize the powerful simplicity of the words of Jesus to love God, love others, and see others become His followers (Matthew 22:37–40, Matthew 28:19–20).

THE GREAT COMMANDMENT NETWORK IS SERVED THROUGH THE FOLLOWING:

Relationship Press – This team collaborates, supports, and joins together with churches, denominational partners, and professional associates to develop, print, and produce resources that facilitate ongoing Great Commandment ministry.

The Center for Relational Leadership – Their mission is to teach, train, and mentor both ministry and corporate leaders in Great Commandment principles, seeking to equip leaders with relational skills so they might lead as Jesus led.

The Galatians 6:6 Retreat Ministry – This ministry offers a unique two-day retreat for ministers and their spouses for personal renewal and for reestablishing and affirming ministry and family priorities.

The Center for Relational Care (CRC) – The CRC provides therapy and support to relationships in crisis through an accelerated process of growth and healing, including Relational Care Intensives for couples, families, and singles.

For more information on how you, your church, ministry, denomination, or movement can be served by the Great Commandment Network write or call:

Great Commandment Network
2511 South Lakeline Blvd.
Cedar Park, Texas 78613
#800-881-8008
Or visit our website: www.GreatCommandment.net

Appendix 2

A SPIRIT-EMPOWERED FAITH

Expresses Itself in Great Commission Living
Empowered by Great Commandment Love

 begins with the end in mind:
The Great Commission calls us
to make disciples.

"Go therefore and make disciples of all the nations, baptizing them in
the name of the Father and the Son and the Holy Spirit teaching them
to observe all things that I have commanded you; and lo, I am with
you always, even to the end of the age." (Matthew 28:19–20)

The ultimate goal of our faith journey is to relate to the person of Jesus,
because it is our relational connection to Jesus that will produce Christlikeness and spiritual growth. This relational perspective of discipleship is
required if we hope to have a faith that is marked by the Spirit's power.

Models of discipleship that are based solely upon what we *know* and
what we *do* are incomplete, lacking the empowerment of a life of loving and
living intimately with Jesus. **A Spirit-empowered faith is relational and**
impossible to realize apart from a special work of the Spirit. For example, the Spirit-empowered outcome of "listening to and hearing God" implies
relationship—it is both relational in focus and requires the Holy Spirit's
power to live.

 begins at the right place:
The Great Commandment calls us to
start with loving God and loving others.

"'You shall love the LORD your God with all your heart, with all your soul,
and with all your mind.' This is the first and great commandment.
And the second is like it: 'You shall love your neighbor as yourself.'
On these two commandments hang all the Law and the Prophets."
(Matthew 22:37–40)

Relevant discipleship does not begin with doctrines or teaching, parables or stewardship—but with loving the Lord with all your heart, mind, soul, and strength and then loving the people closest to you. Since Matthew 22:37–40 gives us the first and greatest commandment, *a Spirit-empowered faith starts where the Great Commandment tells us to start: A disciple must first learn to deeply love the Lord and to express His love to the "nearest ones"—his or her family, church, and community (and in that order).*

 embraces a relational process of Christlikeness.

Scripture reminds us that there are three sources of light for our journey: Jesus, His Word, and His people. The process of discipleship (or becoming more like Jesus) occurs as we relate intimately with each source of light.

"Walk while you have the light, lest darkness overtake you." (John 12:35)

Spirit-empowered discipleship will require a lifestyle of:
* Fresh encounters with Jesus (John 8:12)
* Frequent experiences of Scripture (Psalm 119:105)
* Faithful engagement with God's people (Matthew 5:14)

 can be defined with observable outcomes using a biblical framework.

The metrics for measuring Spirit-empowered faith or the growth of a disciple come from Scripture and are organized/framed around four distinct dimensions of a disciple who serves.

A Spirit-Empowered Faith

And He Himself gave some to be apostles, some prophets,
some evangelists, and some pastors and teachers,
for the equipping of the saints for the work of ministry,
for the edifying of the body of Christ.
(Ephesians 4:11-12)

A relational framework for organizing Spirit-Empowered Discipleship Outcomes draws from a cluster analysis of several Greek (*diakoneo, leitourgeo, douleuo*) and Hebrew words (*'abad, Sharat*), which elaborate on the Ephesians 4:12 declaration that Christ's followers are to be equipped for works of ministry or service. Therefore, the 40 Spirit-Empowered Faith Outcomes have been identified and organized around:

- Serving/loving the Lord – *While they were **ministering** to the Lord and fasting* (Acts 13:2 NASB).[1]
- Serving/loving the Word – *But we will devote ourselves to prayer and to the **ministry** of the word* (Acts 6:4 NASB).[2]
- Serving/loving people – *Through love **serve** one another* (Galatians 5:13 NASB).[3]
- Serving/loving His mission – *Now all these things are from God, who reconciled us to Himself through Christ and gave us the **ministry** of reconciliation* (2 Corinthians 5:18 NASB).[4]

1 Ferguson, David L. *Great Commandment Principle*. Cedar Park, Texas: Relationship Press, 2013.

2 Ferguson, David L. *Relational Foundations*. Cedar Park, Texas: Relationship Press, 2004.

3 Ferguson, David L. *Relational Discipleship*. Cedar Park, Texas: Relationship Press, 2005.

4 "Spirit Empowered Outcomes," www.empowered21.com, Empowered 21 Global Council, http://empowered21.com/discipleship-materials/.

Appendix 3

A SPIRIT-EMPOWERED DISCIPLE LOVES THE LORD THROUGH

L1. Practicing thanksgiving in all things
Enter into His gates with thanksgiving (Ps. 100:4). *In everything give thanks* (1 Th. 5:18). *As sorrowful, yet always rejoicing* (2 Cor. 6:10).

L2. Listening to and hearing God for direction and discernment
"Speak, Lord, for Your servant hears" (1 Sam. 3:8–9). *Mary, who also sat at Jesus' feet and heard His word* (Lk. 10:38–42). *And the Lord said, "Shall I hide from Abraham what I am doing … ?"* (Gen. 18:17). *But as the same anointing teaches you concerning all things …* (1 Jn. 2:27).

L3. Experiencing God as He really is through deepened intimacy with Him
"Hear, O Israel: The Lord our God, the Lord is one! You shall love the Lord your God with all your heart, with all your soul, and with all your strength" (Deut. 6:4–5). *Therefore the Lord will wait, that He may be gracious to you; and therefore He will be exalted, that He may have mercy on you. For the Lord is a God of justice …* (Is. 30:18). See also John 14:9.

L4. Rejoicing regularly in my identity as "His Beloved"
And his banner over me was love (Song of Sol. 2:4). *To the praise of the glory of His grace, by which He made us accepted in the Beloved* (Eph. 1:6). *For so He gives His beloved sleep* (Ps. 127:2).

L5. Living with a passionate longing for purity and to please Him in all things
Who may ascend into the hill of the Lord? … He who has clean hands and a pure heart (Ps. 24:3–4). *Beloved, let us cleanse ourselves from all filthiness of flesh and spirit, perfecting holiness in the fear of God* (2 Cor. 7:1). *"I always do those things that please Him"* (Jn. 8:29). *"Though He slay me, yet will I trust Him"* (Job 13:15).

L6. Consistent practice of self-denial, fasting, and solitude rest

He turned and said to Peter, "Get behind me, Satan! You are offense to Me, for you are not mindful of the things of God, but the things of men" (Mt. 16:23). "But you, when you fast …" (Mt. 6:17). "Be still, and know that I am God" (Ps. 46:10).

L7. Entering often into Spirit-led praise and worship

Bless the LORD, O my soul, and all that is within me (Ps. 103:1). Serve the LORD with fear (Ps. 2:11). I thank You, Father, Lord of heaven and earth (Mt. 11:25).

L8. Disciplined, bold, and believing prayer

Praying always with all prayer and supplication in the Spirit (Eph. 6:18). "Call to Me, and I will answer you" (Jer. 33:3). If we ask anything according to His will, He hears us. And if we know that He hears us, whatever we ask, we know that we have the petitions that we have asked of Him (1 Jn. 5:14–15).

L9. Faithful stewardship and exercise of the gifts of the Spirit for empowered living and sacrifice

By one Spirit we were all baptized into one body—whether Jews or Greeks, whether slaves or free—and have all been made to drink into one Spirit (1 Cor. 12:13). "But you shall receive power when the Holy Spirit has come upon you" (Acts 1:8). But the manifestation of the Spirit is given to each one for the profit of all (1 Cor. 12:7). See also 1 Pet. 4:10 and Rom. 12:6.

L10. Practicing the presence of the Lord, yielding to the Spirit's work of Christlikeness

But we all, with unveiled face, … are being transformed into the same from glory to glory, just as by the Spirit of the Lord (2 Cor. 3:18). As the deer pants for the water brooks, so pants my soul after You, O God (Ps. 42:1).

A SPIRIT-EMPOWERED DISCIPLE LIVES THE WORD THROUGH

W1. Frequently being led by the Spirit into deeper love for the One who wrote the Word

" 'You shall love the Lord your God … .' 'You shall love neighbor as yourself.' On these two commandments hang all the Law and the Prophets" (Mt. 22:37–40). And I will delight myself in Your commandments, which I love. (Ps. 119:47). "The fear of the Lord is clean … . More to be desired are they than gold … sweeter also than honey" (Ps. 19:9–10).

W2. Being a "living epistle" in reverence and awe as His Word becomes real in my life, vocation, and calling

You are our epistle written in our hearts, known and read by all men (2 Cor. 3:2). And the Word became flesh and dwelt among us (Jn. 1:14). Husbands, love your wives … cleanse her with the washing of water by the word (Eph. 5:25–26). See also Tit. 2:5. And whatever you do, do it heartily, as to the Lord and not to men (Col. 3:23).

W3. Yielding to the Scripture's protective cautions and transforming power to bring life change in me

Through Your precepts I get understanding; therefore I hate every false way (Ps. 119:104). "Let it be to me according to your word" (Lk. 1:38). How can a young man cleanse his way? By taking heed according to Your word (Ps. 119:9). See also Col. 3:16–17.

W4. Humbly and vulnerably sharing of the Spirit's transforming work through the Word

I will speak of your testimonies also before kings, and will not be ashamed (Ps. 119:46). Preach the word! Be ready in season and out of season (2 Tim. 4:2).

W5. Meditating consistently on more and more of the Word hidden in the heart

Your word I have hidden in my heart, that I might not sin against You (Ps. 119:11). *Let the words of my mouth and the meditation of my heart be acceptable in Your sight, O LORD, my strength and my Redeemer* (Ps. 19:14).

W6. Encountering Jesus in the Word for deepened transformation in Christlikeness

But we all, with unveiled face, … are being transformed into the same image from glory to glory, just as by the Spirit of the Lord (2 Cor. 3:18). *If you abide in Me, and My words abide in you, you will ask what you desire, and it shall be done for you* (Jn. 15:7). See also Lk. 24:32, Ps. 119:136, and 2 Cor. 1:20.

W7. A life explained as one of "experiencing Scripture"

But this is what was spoken by the prophet Joel (Acts 2:16). *This is my comfort in my affliction, for Your word has given me life* (Ps. 119:50). *My soul breaks with longing for Your judgements at all times* (Ps. 119:20).

W8. Living "naturally supernatural" in all of life as His Spirit makes the written Word (*logos*) the living Word (*rhema*)

So then aith comes by hearing, and hearing by the word (rhema) of God (Rom. 10:17). *Your word is a lamp to my feet and a light to my path* (Ps. 119:105).

W9. Living abundantly "in the present" as His Word brings healing to hurt and anger, guilt, fear, and condemnation—which are heart hindrances to life abundant

"The thief does not come except to steal, and to kill, and to destroy" (Jn. 10:10). *I will run the course of Your commandments, for You shall enlarge my heart* (Ps. 119:32). *"And you shall know the truth, and the truth shall make you free"* (Jn. 8:32). *Stand fast therefore in the liberty by which Christ has made us free, and do not be entangled again with a yoke of bondage* (Gal. 5:1).

W10. Implicit, unwavering trust that His Word will never fail
"The grass withers, the flower fades, but the word of our God stands forever" (Is. 40:8). *"So shall My word be that goes forth from My mouth; it shall not return to Me void"* (Is. 55:11).

A SPIRIT-EMPOWERED DISCIPLE LOVES PEOPLE THROUGH

P1. Living a Spirit-led life of doing good in all of life: relationships and vocation, community and calling
Who went about doing good … (Acts 10:38). *"Let your light so shine before men, that they may see your good works and glorify your Father in heaven"* (Mt. 5:16). *"But love your enemies, do good, and lend, hoping for nothing in return; and your reward will be great, and you will be sons of the Most High. For He is kind to the unthankful and evil"* (Lk. 6:35). See also Rom. 15:2.

P2. "Startling people" with loving initiatives to "give first"
"Give, and it will be given to you: good measure, pressed down, shaken together, and running over will be put into your bosom" (Lk. 6:38). *Then Jesus said, "Father, forgive them, for they do not know what they do"* (Lk. 23:34). See also Lk. 23:43 and Jn. 19:27.

P3. Discerning the relational needs of others with a heart to give of His love
Let no corrupt word proceed out of your mouth, but what is good for necessary edification, that it might impart grace to the hearers (Eph. 4:29). *And my God shall supply all your need according to His riches in glory by Christ Jesus* (Phil. 4:19). See also Lk. 6:30.

P4. Seeing people as needing BOTH redemption from sin AND intimacy in relationships, addressing both human fallen-ness and aloneness
But God demonstrates His own love toward us, in that while we were still sinners, Christ died for us (Rom. 5:8). *And when Jesus came to the place, He looked up and saw him, and said to him, "Zacchaeus, make haste and come down, for today I must stay at your house"* (Lk. 19:5). See also Mk. 8:24 and Gen. 2:18.

P5. Ministering His life and love to our nearest ones at home and with family as well as faithful engagement in His body, the church
Husbands, likewise, dwell with them with understanding, giving honor to the wife, as to the weaker vessel, and as being heirs together of the grace of life, that your prayers may not be hindered (1 Pet. 3:7). See also 1 Pet. 3:1 and Ps. 127:3.

P6. Expressing the fruit of the Spirit as a lifestyle and identity
But the fruit of the Spirit is love, joy, peace, longsuffering, kindness, goodness, faithfulness, gentleness, self-control (Gal. 5:22–23). *A man's stomach shall be satisfied from the fruit of his mouth; From the produce of his lips he shall be filled* (Prov. 18:20).

P7. Expecting and demonstrating the supernatural as His spiritual gifts are made manifest and His grace is at work by His Spirit
In mighty signs and wonders, by the power of the Spirit of God, so that from Jerusalem and round about to Illyricum I have fully preached the gospel of Christ (Rom. 15:19). *"Most assuredly, I say to you, he who believes in Me, the works that I do he will do also"* (Jn. 14:12). See also 1 Cor. 14:1.

P8. Taking courageous initiative as a peacemaker, reconciling relationships along life's journey
Be at peace among yourselves (1 Th. 5:13). *For He Himself is our peace, who has made both one, and has broken down the middle wall of separation* (Eph. 2:14). *Confess your trespasses to one another, and pray for one another, that you may be healed* (Jas. 5:16).

P9. Demonstrating His love to an ever growing network of "others" as He continues to challenge us to love "beyond our comfort"

He who says, "I know Him," and does not keep His commandments, is a liar, and the truth is not in him (1 Jn. 2:4). If someone says, "I love God," and hates his brother, he is a liar; for he who does not love his brother whom he has seen, how can he love God whom he has not seen? (1 Jn. 4:20).

P10. Humbly acknowledging to the Lord, ourselves, and others that it is Jesus in and through us who is loving others at their point of need

"Take My yoke upon you and learn from Me, for I am gentle and lowly in heart, and you will find rest for your souls" (Mt. 11:29). "If I then, your Lord and Teacher, have washed your feet, you also ought to wash one another's feet" (Jn. 13:14).

A SPIRIT-EMPOWERED DISCIPLE LIVES HIS MISSION THROUGH

M1. Imparting the gospel and one's very life in daily activities and relationships, vocation and community

So, affectionately longing for you, we were well pleased to impart to you not only the gospel of God, but also our own lives, because you had become dear to us (1 Th. 2:8–9). See also Eph. 6:19.

M2. Expressing and extending the kingdom of God as compassion, |justice, love, and forgiveness are shared

"I must preach the kingdom of God to the other cities also, because for this purpose I have been sent" (Lk. 4:43). "As You sent Me into the world, I also have sent them into the world" (Jn. 17:18). Restore to me the joy of Your salvation, and uphold me by Your generous Spirit. Then I will teach transgressors Your ways, and sinners shall be converted to You (Ps. 51:12–13). See also Mic. 6:8.

M3. Championing Jesus as the only hope of eternal life and abundant living

"Nor is there salvation in any other, for there is no other name under heaven given among men by which we must be saved" (Acts 4:12). *"The thief does not come except to steal, and to kill, and to destroy. I have come so that they may have life, and that they have it more abundantly"* (Jn. 10:10). See also Acts 4:12 and Jn. 14:6.

M4. Yielding to the Spirit's role to convict others as He chooses, resisting expressions of condemnation

"And when He has come, He will convict the world of sin, and of righteousness, and of judgment" (Jn. 16:8). *Who is he who condemns? It is Christ who died, and furthermore is also risen, who is even at the right hand of God, who also makes intercession for us* (Rom. 8:34). See also Rom. 8:1.

M5. Ministering His life and love to the "least of these"

"Then He will answer them saying, 'Assuredly, I say to you inasmuch as you did not do it to one of the least of these, you did not do it to Me'" (Mt. 25:45). *Pure and undefiled religion before God and the Father is this: to visit orphans and widows in their trouble, and to keep oneself unspotted from the world* (Jas. 1:27).

M6. Bearing witness of a confident peace and expectant hope in God's lordship in all things

Now may the Lord of peace Himself give you peace always in every way. The Lord be with you all (2 Thess. 3:16). *And let the peace of God rule in your hearts, to which also you were called in one body; and be thankful* (Col. 3:15). See also Rom. 8:28 and Ps. 146:5.

M7. Faithfully sharing of time, talent, gifts, and resources in furthering His mission

Of which I became a minister according to the stewardship from God which was given to me for you, to fulfill the word of God (Col. 1:25). *"For everyone to whom much is given, from him much will be required"* (Lk. 12:48). See also 1 Cor. 4:1–2.

M8. Attentive listening to others' story, vulnerably sharing of our story, and a sensitive witness of Jesus' story as life's ultimate hope; developing your story of prodigal, preoccupied and pain-filled living; listening for others' story and sharing Jesus' story

But sanctify the Lord God in your hearts, and always be ready to give a defense to everyone who asks you a reason for the hope that is in you, with meekness and fear (1 Pet. 3:15). *"For this my son was dead and is alive again"* (Luke 15:24). See also Mk. 5:21–42 and Jn. 9:1–35.

M9. Pouring our life into others, making disciples who in turn make disciples of others

"Go therefore and make disciples of all the nations, baptizing them in the name of the Father and of the Son and of the Holy Spirit, teaching them to observe all things that I commanded you; and lo, I am with you always, even to the end of the age" (Mt. 28:19–20). See also 2 Tim. 2:2.

M10. Living submissively within His body, the Church, as instruction and encouragement; reproof and correction are graciously received by faithful disciples

Submitting to one another in the fear of God (Eph. 5:21). *Brethren, if a man is overtaken in any trespass, you who are spiritual restore such a one in a spirit of gentleness, considering yourself lest you also be tempted* (Gal. 6:1). See also Gal. 6:2.

We pray God has used
Revival Now: A Jesus Awakening
to set your heart on fire for
true revival from Jesus.

For more from the *Jesus
Now Awakening Series*,
check out the first book in
the series, *Jesus Now: God
is Up to Something Big*, by
Tom Phillips.

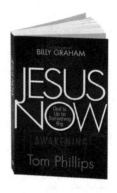